C000069253

not a guide to

Leeds

Diane Holloway

First published 2012

The History Press
The Mill, Brimscombe Port
Stroud, Gloucestershire, GL5 2QG
www.thehistorypress.co.uk

British Library Cataloguing in Publication Data.
A catalogue record for this book is available from the British Library.

ISBN 978 0 7524 7656 8

Typesetting and origination by The History Press
Printed in Great Britain

Coat of Arms

The stars are from the coat of arms of Sir Thomas Danby, first mayor of Leeds.

*

The fleece signifies the wool industry, which was the bedrock of wealth in the city.

*

The owls are from the coat of arms of Sir John Saville, first alderman of Leeds.

*

The Latin motto, *Pro Rege et Lege*, means 'For King and Law'.

Contents

Origin of Leeds

Leeds has variously been called Loides, Loidis, Ledes and Leedes.

Loides was possibly the name of a tribe and could mean 'people of the flowing river', a reference to the River Aire. A saint called Cadroe is said to have visited two kings in Loides whose boundaries met there.

Modern-day Leeds would have been part of an ancient kingdom of Elmet. Leeds could have been a Roman settlement, as Roman and Brigante remains have been found in the vicinity. The name 'Leeds' is from the Anglo-Saxon name Loidis. In *Historia Ecclesiastica*, Bede states, in a discussion regarding the location of an altar from a church erected by Edwin, great uncle of Hilda, Abbess of Whitby, '*I regione quae vocatur Loidis*' (in the region known as Leeds).

Elmet survived well after the coming of the Anglo-Saxons. Originally, Loidis was the name of a forest in the kingdom of Elmet.

An eleventh-century manuscript claimed that, in the tenth century, Loidis lay on the boundary between the Viking kingdom of Jorvik and the Welsh-speaking kingdom of Strathclyde (which included Lancashire, Cumbria and south-western Scotland).

The history of Leeds can be traced back to AD 627 when, according to the Venerable Bede in 730, 'It was a place where Kings built themselves a Country-Seat'.

Leeds was destined to become one of the most famous wool-making centres in the country, and the cottage-craft businesses of weaving and spinning developed steadily during the Middle Ages.

Maps Through the Ages

Here is Leeds in 1725 (opposite above) and 1866 (opposite below).

The oldest surviving church is St John's in Briggate. Briggate is the point from which Leeds evolved from a tiny village to a thriving city.

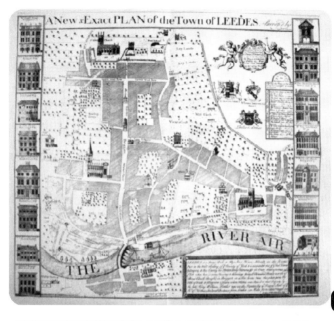

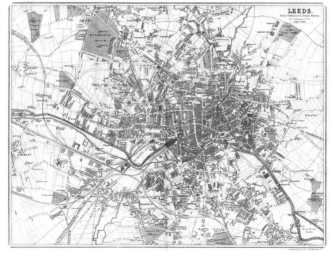

9

Street Names

The street names in Leeds revolve mainly around the heritage of the city.

However, there is one name that is baffling but delightful: **Daffels Road, Grange** and **Avenue**, plus **Daffels Wood** close by. Perhaps someone got mixed up with the spelling, and there was once an extensive daffodil plantation in this area – who knows? A more haunting street name, which leaves little to the imagination, is **Hangingstone Road**.

Two of the oldest roads in Leeds are **Kirkgate** and **Briggate**: road to the church (Kirk) and the road to the bridge (Brig).

De Lacy (Street/Lane/Mount) denotes the city's first Norman overlord.

Lascelles/Harewood (Place/Road/Terrace etc.) shows an affiliation with the Lascelles family at Harewood House.

Asquith (Avenue/Close/Drive) displays pride in a son of Leeds who became Prime Minister.

Aire (Mount/Close/Place/Street and Road) shows the dependence Leeds once had on the River Aire.

Vesper (Rise/Road/Gardens and Gate) demonstrates continued links with nearby Kirkstall Abbey.

Templar Street and **Temple** (Park/Gardens/Road/Rise/Lane and Drive) relate to the famous Knights Templar.

Lastly, there is **Pepper Road**, in the shadow of four blast furnaces, where smoke and sulphur coloured the bricks of surrounding houses red.

Villages Leeds has 'Swallowed'

The city of Leeds has, over the years, swallowed up many of the outlying villages, particularly in the mid-nineteenth century when industry really took Leeds forward as a major city.

Over the years many of these villages have lost their identity. However, if one looks closely there remains the odd reminder of how things used to be. Suburbs have been pushed ever outwards, and once leafy villages on the outskirts of Leeds (Horsforth still thinks it is) are now very much part of the metropolis.

Bramley was home to Leeds market during the plague of 1644/45.

Holbeck was the cradle of the Industrial Revolution.

Headingly was at the centre of a wapentake named Skyrack.

Horsforth is an Anglo-Saxon 'horse ford' for the River Aire.

Meanwood was the site of a civil-war skirmish.

Farsley received the first shipment of Merino wool from Australia to be made into a coat for King George III.

Wortley was home to a 'roundhouse' used for servicing locomotives.

The suburbs are 6 to 8 miles out of Leeds centre, and include places such as **Bramhope**, **Aberford**, **Harewood**, **Roundhay**, **Adel**, **Wetherby**, **Ardsley**.

Distance from Leeds

	Km	Miles
Harvey Nichols, Sloane Sq., London	339	211
Jenners Store, Edinburgh	335	208
Commercial Centre, Paris, France	780	485
Commercial Centre, London	340	212
Sears/Skydeck Tower, Chicago, USA	6,232	3,873
Maxwell Street Market, Chicago, USA	6,235	3,875
Old Bus Depot Market, Canberra, Australia	16,930	9,142
Mugga-Mugga cottage, Canberra, Australia	16,951	9,157
Burj Khalifa, world's tallest building, Dubai	5,615	3,490
Gold Souk, Dubai	5,615	3,490
Raffles Hotel, Singapore	10,941	6,840
Island of Sentosa, via cable car, Singapore	10,900	6,855
Cristo de la Concordia statue, Cochabamba, Bolivia	10,013	6,223
Cassidy and Sundance's final resting place, Tupiza, Bolivia	10,372	6,446
Victoria Memorial, Calcutta, India	8,005	4,975
Dakshinswar Kali Temple, Calcutta, India	8,005	4,975
Caerphilly Castle, Wales	364	226
Citadel of Aleppo, Syria	3,556	2,209

Leeds Windmills

There are at least seven remaining windmills in Leeds. A few more may well survive in one form or another (dereliction being the most common), though none are still in use as mills.

The earliest reference to a windmill in Leeds was in the Domesday Book of 1086 at Hillam, but both village and mill are no more. This particular mill was water-powered from the Cock Beck and was shown on a 1775 map. As far back as 1185, the Knights Templar owned two corn mills and one fulling mill at Temple Newsam, on the River Aire. By 1258, Edmund de Lacy had two mills on his 90 acres of arable land. Most of the mills in the Leeds area were corn mills, constructed as 'Tower' mills rather than 'Post' mills.

The post mill on the opposite page has been incorporated into a hotel on the York Road. Yet another has been converted into living accommodation and is surrounded by a housing estate and a third, which is in a lovely, tranquil setting, has also been converted into a home. There are others dotted about the area, some of which are in residential use.

Statues Around Leeds

Leeds is full of statues. Here are just a few:

Leeds City Centre
Cheltenham House, South Parade, has a frieze depicting early trading links showing packers, porters, American Indians, Arabs and a prospector.

City Square is home to a statue of the Black Prince on horseback by Thomas Brock. It also has a statue of Dr Walter Hook (Bishop of Leeds), by F.W. Pomeroy, a likeness of Joseph Priestley by Alfred Drury, a James Watt by H.C. Fehr and a John Harrison (benefactor and mayor of Leeds), also by H.C. Fehr.

Park Square is home to Circe with Two Swine by Alfred Drury.

City Art Gallery, The Headrow, has the famous Reclining Woman by Henry Moore.

Bond Court is home to A Yorkshire Family Watching a Frenchman Play Boule by Roger Burnett.

Dortmund Square is home to The Drayman by Arthur Shulze-Engles.

Merrion Centre is the site of Androgyne by Glen Hellman.

Leighton Street depicts The Human Spirit by Faith Babbington.

Opposite **Leeds University** you will find the Duke of Wellington, by Baron Carlo Marochetti.

Eastgate roundabout is home to Arthur Aaron (bomber pilot) by Graham Ibbeson.

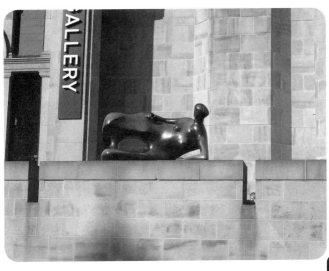

Hyde Park, Woodhouse Moor is home to the Queen Victoria memorial by George Frampton. The Queen Victoria memorial sculpture is one of many memorials erected after her death in 1901; she bears an orb and a book. The four female figures around the base depict her four main dominions. Hyde Park is also home to Sir Robert Peel by William Behnes. Robert Peel, as Home Secretary, created the 'Peeler' in 1829 – and thus began the police force as we know it today. He died in a riding accident in 1850, and twenty-six statues of him were erected around Britain. The one in Leeds claimed to be the first, and also claims to be the first bronze figure in Britain that was cast in one piece. Some sources also believe that he was the first statue to be dressed as his contemporaries would have known him, rather than in Greek or Roman drapery.

Woodhouse Moor is home to a statue of Henry Marsden, mayor of Leeds and founder of the Leeds Music Festival, by John Throp.

Woodhouse Square also has a statue of Sir Peter Fairbairn by Matthew Noble. Queen Victoria stayed at his house when she opened Leeds Town Hall; she knighted him at this time.

Animal Statues

Around the refurbished Leeds Waterfront are a number of animal sculptures executed in metal. Assumed to have been commissioned by Leeds City Council, by various artists, they are:

Brewery Wharfe: A heron.

Leeds Waterfront: Two birds in flight and a dragonfly.

Town Hall: Lions by William Keyworth.

Park Row: Rearing black horse by Peter Tysoe.

City Square: Seagulls in flight. Executed in bronze, the seagulls symbolize a future on the rise for the Norwich Union building, which was designed by Abbey Hanson Rowe in 1996.

Twinned Towns

Nothing is new, or so the saying goes – and thus it is with town twinning. The tradition began centuries ago between Germany and France. The modern idea began in the 1920s, the concept gaining in popularity after the Second World War. This is seen as an effort to forge links through cultural and commercial enterprises.

Leeds is twinned with:

1967 – **Siegen, Germany**. This link concentrates on high-school language links and sharing memories between older residents.

1968 – **Lille, France**: share input on education and sharing memories of the older residents.

1969 – **Brno, Czech Republic**: centres on education and business.

1990 – **Hangzhue, Zhejiang Province, China**: the links here are culture and business.

1998 – **Durban, South Africa**: works with sports and primary schools.

2007 – **Louisville, USA**: focuses on the arts and culture.

2009 – Marked the fortieth anniversary of the Leeds partnership with **Dortmund, Germany**.

Leeds has further links with: Ballina, Ireland; Barcelona, Spain; Brasor, Romania; Colombo, Sri Lanka; Dnipropetrovsk, Ukraine; Nis, Serbia; and Saint Mary, Jamaica.

Worldwide Leeds

Leeds can be found all over the world, including:

Leeds, Alabama

Leeds, Utah

Leeds, North Dakota

Leeds, New York

Leeds, Maine

Leeds, Massachusetts

Leeds, Missouri

Leeds, South Carolina

Leeds, Wisconsin

Leeds, Maryland

Leeds, Iowa

Leeds, Illinois

Leeds, Jamaica (Saint Elizabeth)

Leeds, South Africa (Northern Cape)

Leeds, Guyana (East Berbice-Corentyne)

Leeds, United Kingdom (Kent)

And last but not least, Leeds County, Canada, founded in 1792, and joined with Grenville County in 1850. The county took its name from Francis Osbourne, 5th Duke of Leeds (Yorkshire).

Historical Timeline

Leeds, a small village with a population of around 200, appears in the Domesday Book belonging to the Norman Baron Ilbert de Lacy.

A free grammar school is founded in Leeds.

During the civil war Royalists capture Leeds: the town then changes hands another three times.

Kirkstall Abbey is founded by Henry de Lacy.

Leeds Market begins to operate.

The Farnley Wood Plot. Plotters meet to overthrow King Charles II.

1086   1152   1258   1552   1642   1663

1139   1207   1399   1626   1662

King Stephen besieges the de Lacy Castle on Mill Hill (roughly where City Square is now) on his way to Scotland.

King Richard is briefly imprisoned in de Lacy Castle in Leeds.

Second charter, this time by King Charles II, gives Leeds a mayor.

Maurice Paynall, known as Maurice De Gant, the lord of the manor, turns Leeds into a small market town.

King Charles I grants Royal Charter of Incorporation, which established Leeds as a borough with the election of the first alderman and burgesses.

Grand Theatre is built. Thornton's Arcade is built.

Cholera kills more than 2,000 people.

In March, bombing kills seventy-seven people in Leeds.

Leeds mob attacks John Wesley.

The famous domed Corn Exchange is built.

Leeds becomes a city by Royal Charter.

1745   1849   1861   1878   1893   1941

1699   1816   1859   1872   1884   1904   2002

Canal completed; Leeds is linked to Liverpool.

Horse-drawn trams run in the streets. The first public library opens.

Leeds University is founded.

The Aire and Calder rivers are made navigable, linking Leeds with the Ouse, Humber and the sea.

Leeds Rifles are raised.

Michael Marks (of Marks & Spencer) begins trading in Leeds.

Queen Elizabeth II visits Leeds for Golden Jubilee.

Freak Weather in Leeds

1816 – The year without a summer, when a volcanic eruption in Tambora, East Indies, left the North of England unusually cold.

1947 – In March, people skated on the River Wharfe – for the first time in fifty years.

1958 – Earth tremors felt in Leeds.

1962 – Gale-force winds, resulting in 60,000 homes damaged in Leeds.

1962-63 – Winter freeze lasts for three months.

1976 – The hot summer brings worst drought since 1720.

1990 – On 30 April, Leeds was the warmest place in Britain.

1991 – Floods hit suburbs of Leeds, with the Wharfe bursting its banks.

2000 – August hailstorm hits Leeds area with nearly an inch of hail in places; trees block roads and lorries are blown over. In November, temperatures rose to 17°C.

2007 – Floods, lightning and a tornado bring Leeds to a standstill.

Demographics

The thirtieth most populous city in the European Union, and fourth most populous urban sub-division in England, Leeds' urban sub-division is 109 square km, or 42 square miles.

Population:	764,561
White British	637,800
Pakistani community	15,064
Bangladeshi community	2,537
Indian	12,303
Chinese	3,447
Black Caribbean	6,720
Mixed heritage	9,700
Other groups	78,000
Leeds city region	2.9 million

Denomination

Christian	72.1 per cent
Jewish	16.8 per cent
Muslim	3.0 per cent
Sikh	0.5 per cent
Non religious	8.1 per cent

Leeds Quotations

'We're funny from the North, Pete. What do we care about Brighton? Bloody Southerners. Look where we are!'
On Leeds in *The Damned United*, 2009, David Peace

'Ye can't be going off to Leeds until ye are older, I am thinking.'
***A Woman of Substance*, Barbara Taylor Bradford**

'"Lots of things!" She exclaimed pithily, and threw him a scathing look. "The Bank, that's what. Ham and Shank. The Bank. See. It rhymes. Rhyming slang we calls it in Leeds."'
***A Woman of Substance*, Barbara Taylor Bradford**

'The trial had lasted for eighteen days, and from the moment the judge had entered the courtroom the public benches had been filled to overflowing. The jury at Leeds Crown Court had been out for almost two days, and rumour had it that they were hopelessly divided.'
***Twelve Red Herrings*, Jeffrey Archer**

'I longed to go where there was life.'
Charlotte Bronte on Leeds, 1847

'I have never had the faintest illusion about Leeds…'
G.K. Chesterton

'Leeds may look dark on the outside, but inside it is full of colour and warmth.'
John Betjeman

'Leeds is not an easy city to understand. It does not give an immediate impression or quickly reveal its character.'
Patrick Nuttgens, architectural historian

'A book is a device to ignite the imagination.'
Alan Bennett, Leeds playwright

'A jazz musician is a juggler who uses harmonies instead of oranges.'
Benny Green, Leeds-born musician

Awards for Leeds

Leeds is a northern city success story. Once a large and noisy industrial metropolis, it has, over the last fifteen to twenty years, morphed into a vibrant, lively and colourful city.

The local economy has strengthened immensely, and now Leeds is one of the premier destinations for business, students and visitors alike. Leeds has been marked out as a city full of confidence, hard work a byword in the city; as such, it has received many awards and accolades. Here are just a few of the awards that have marked out Leeds as head and shoulders above the rest:

Marketing Excellence Award, 2011

Leeds City Sanctuary Award, 2011

UK's Favourite City Award (*Condé Nast Traveller* magazine), 2011

Britain's Best City for Business Award, 2011

Visitor City of the Year, 2011

Best UK University Destination, 2011

Number One City for Clubbing Award, 2011

National Youth Agency Award, 2010

Both the Corn Exchange and the Henry Moore Institute have won RIBA awards (Royal Institute of British Architects)

Royal Visits

1858 – Queen Victoria opened Leeds Town Hall. A competition was held in 1851 and was won by a then-unknown architect, Cuthbert Brodrick FRIBA. He was also responsible for two other iconic buildings in Leeds, the Corn Exchange and the Mechanics Institute, now Leeds City Museum.

1872 – Prince Arthur opened Roundhay Park. Today, this wonderful park has added attractions, including a Tropical Garden, second only to Kew Gardens, a Butterfly House and a Desert House with a family of meerkats.

1908 – King Edward VII opened new university buildings and granted the university its own charter as an independent institution.

1933 – King George V and Queen Mary opened the new Civic Hall. It was designed by Vincent Harris, and was built at a cost of £360,000. It provided much-needed jobs in Leeds at a time of depression in the country.

1958 – The Queen and Duke of Edinburgh visited during the centenary of the Leeds Music Festival at the Town Hall. It was the young Queen's first visit to Leeds after her coronation. Benjamin Britten's Op 60 was premiered before the Queen and Prince Philip.

1973 – Queen Elizabeth, the Queen Mother, granted freedom of the city to HMS *Ark Royal*.

2007 – Princess Royal opened the refurbished Tiled Hall as part of the Leeds City Art Gallery and Library.

Benefactors of Leeds

Propelling Leeds into the Industrial Revolution were:

Benjamin Gott: His Armley Mills factory was once the largest factory in the world. He reinvested money for the benefit of his employees. The grounds to his house are now a public park and golf course.

John Harrison: Endowed Leeds Grammar School and St John's church. Invented the marine chronometer, which established the longitude of a ship at sea. It had seemed an intractable problem – so much so that the British Government offered a prize of £20,000 (£2.87 million today) for finding a resolution to the difficulty.

John Hives: A flax manufacturer; his mill, Banks Mill, on the River Aire, used 600,000 gallons of water per day.

John Marshall: He built the innovative flax-spinning Marshalls Mill. It was modelled on an Egyptian-style temple, and has model sheep grazing on the roof.

Matthew Murray: An engine and machine-tool manufacturer, Murray designed and built the first commercially viable steam locomotive. He was an innovative designer in many fields and set up his own factory, supplying machinery to the mills in Leeds.

Joseph Priestley: He was a Presbyterian minister, liberal educator and scientist and discovered the properties of oxygen. He counted Benjamin Franklin among his friends.

John Smeaton: He was one of the first people to call himself an engineer. His multi-skilled approach to problems marked him out as a pioneer in engineering. Smeaton's name is remembered through a community college in Leeds.

Benevolent Beings of Leeds

Thomas Wade and Alice Lodge: The charities of Thomas Wade arise from his will, dated 1530, and that of Alice Lodge's, dated 1638. Wade's Charity is the working name of The Charities of Thomas Wade and Others (as other benefactors later added to the charity).

Margaret Susan Cheshire, Baroness Ryder of Warsaw and Baroness Cheshire, CMG, OBE: Better known as Sue Ryder, Margaret Susan Cheshire is associated with many charitable organisations, most notably the Sue Ryder care homes and charity shops.

Titus Salt: Born in Morely, Titus was the son of a wealthy textile mill owner. After taking over the family firm, he had within twenty years added five more textile mills to the firm. In 1850 he built an industrial community called Saltaire (in a fringe area of Leeds). The most modern in Europe, it included 850 houses for his workers. It was estimated that during his lifetime he gave £500,000 to good causes. However, he objected to the 1833 Government Act to prevent children under the age of nine working in factories and textile mills.

Jane Tomlinson CBE: Studied Mathematics at Leeds University and later trained as a radiographer at Leeds General Infirmary. She raised £1.85 million for children's and cancer charities by completing a series of athletic challenges. 'Run For All' is her legacy. In 2006 Jane spent nine weeks cycling 3,800 miles across the USA, raising £250,000. She died in September 2007 aged forty-three.

Sir Jimmy Savile OBE, KCSG: He joined the BBC in 1968, which was the beginning of a celebrated career on radio and television. He is credited with raising £40 million for charity.

Jimi Heselden: Jimi was a true British entrepreneur. A former coal miner, he made his fortune manufacturing the Hesco bastion, a type of barrier system used as flood control and for military fortifications. He died whilst riding a Segway in 2010. He donated £100,000 to the Leeds Children's Charity and gave £23 million to the Leeds Community Foundation.

Distinguished Folk

Thomas Chippendale

Chippendale first published his collection of furniture in the *Gentleman and Cabinet Maker's Directory* in 1754. The influence of the book was so ubiquitous that the name Chippendale is often indiscriminately applied to mid-eighteenth-century furniture.

Robert Blackburn

Blackburn flew his first monoplane in 1910 from Saltburn; it was made out of wood, fabric and steel plus some brass and string. It crashed. He redesigned it in 1911, at Filey, and it averaged 50mph. He organised flights for the public at Roundhay Park. When he died his company became part of Hawker Siddeley, which later merged into British Aerospace.

Herbert Asquith

Herbert Asquith became Prime Minister in 1908. The failed Battle of Dardanelles in 1915 and the massive casualties of the Somme plus the 1916 Easter Uprising in Dublin all conspired to his fall from grace. The introduction of conscription was not enough to quell dissent against him, which was led by the press who blamed him entirely for the military failures. His failure in wartime overshadowed his successful stewardship in peacetime. Furthermore, intrigue by Lloyd George, who succeeded him as Prime Minister, sealed his fate and he never held office again.

James Henry Atkinson

James Atkinson, an ironmonger from Leeds, invented the mousetrap. It remains the most well-known mousetrap, which slams shut in 30,000ths of a second, a record that has never been beaten. He sold the patent in 1913 for £1,000 to the Proctor Brothers; that company has been manufacturing the trap ever since.

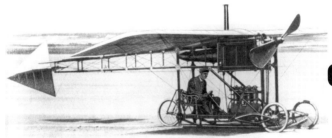

Writers from Leeds

Alan Bennett

One of the most innovative and important playwrights of our time, Alan is very hard to pigeonhole and is seen as a loveable eccentric. His oeuvre includes plays, books, short stories, television dramas and films. He is deeply connected to his Yorkshire roots, often bringing in the dialect to his plays. Notable among his works for television are *An Englishman Abroad* and the *Talking Heads* series; plays include *The Madness of King George III*, which later became a film. His prolific output of books includes *The History Boys* and *The Uncommon Reader*.

Kay Mellor OBE

After graduating from Bretton Hall College, Kay began her career by forming the Yorkshire Theatre Company with two other students, performing plays she had written. By the 1980s she began working for Granada Television writing for the soap opera *Coronation Street* and later wrote several episodes for *Brookside*. She has a host of dramas to her credit, including *A Passionate Woman*, *Between the Sheets*, *The Chase* and *Fat Friends*.

Barbara Taylor Bradford

Starting out in a typing pool at the *Yorkshire Evening Post*; by twenty Barbara was the fashion editor for *Woman's Own* magazine and a journalist on Fleet Street for the *London Evening News*. The year 1979 saw the publication of her first novel, set in her native Leeds, *A Woman of Substance*. She has written a further twenty-seven novels. In 1999, she was the first living female author to be featured on a postage stamp.

Personalities from Leeds

Barry Cryer OBE
A great comedy writer who continues to write and perform his one-man show and is a regular on various radio shows.

John Craven OBE
His career began as a journalist with the *Harrogate Advertiser*. His television career began in 1972 with the children's programme *Newsround* and continues with *Countryfile*.

Jeremy Paxton
Has worked for the BBC since 1977 and is best known as a journalist, author and television presenter.

Vesta Victoria
A famous nineteenth-century music hall singer. Walter Sickert painted her portrait in 1890, and she lived in a houseboat moored near Hampton Court.

Ernie Wise OBE
Met Eric Morecambe at the age of sixteen. The following year he began the famous partnership with Eric, which was to last forty-three years.

Peter O'Toole
After first deciding to be a journalist, he discovered the theatre; the film *Lawrence of Arabia* made him a star.

John Simm
Became a household name playing Sam Tyler in *Life on Mars*.

Gaynor Faye
Has appeared in a string of television shows, most notably *Coronation Street*, *Fat Friends* and *Dancing on Ice*.

Corrine Bailey Rae
Began singing in her local church. She graduated in 2000 from Leeds University. She has sold over five million albums.

Mel B (Brown)
Best known as 'Scary Spice' of the Spice Girls. Now works predominately in America.

Sporting Leeds

A sporting few from Leeds:

Sir Len Hutton
Test cricketer and opening batsman. England captain in 1952 – and in 1953 the team regained the Ashes. He went on to become a Test selector, journalist and broadcaster.

Mike Tindall
This England rugby player is married to Zara, granddaughter of Queen Elizabeth II.

Brian Close
Yorkshire cricket captain, his career lasted from 1948 until 1977. He scored 35,000 runs, which included fifty-two centuries.

Ryan Bailey
Played for Leeds Rhinos and made his debut in the Super League at the age of eighteen and was an England international.

Several Olympians come from Leeds, including:

Kaye Lovatt, swimmer, 1980 Moscow Olympics; **Andrew Astbury,** swimmer, 1980 Moscow Olympics; **Jonny Clay,** cyclist, 2000 Sydney Olympics and **Mick Hill**, javelin, 1988 Seoul, 1992 Barcelona, and 1996 Atlanta.

Leeds University and Leeds Metropolitan University are both hotbeds for training Olympic sportsmen and women, including:

Fiona May, swimmer, 1988 Seoul; **Giles Long MBE,** paralympic swimmer, 1996 Atlanta; **Wilf Paish,** coach for various Olympians, and trained Tessa Sanderson for the javelin; **Norman Hughes,** hockey, 1984 LA; **Simon Mason,** hockey, 1996, 2000, 2004 (the most capped hockey goalkeeper to represent Great Britain).

Sporting Venues

Leeds loyally supports all manner of sporting activities. **The Headingly Stadium** attracts large crowds. The stadium hosts national and international cricket, and both rugby league and rugby union have made it their home-town venue.

Leeds United Football Club was formed in 1904: their ground was, and is still, at **Elland Road**. Election to the football league was in 1905 and is still going strong. The many ups and downs of the club will be well known to football fans, but the club remains strong.

The Leeds Carnegie Sports facility is a breeding ground for young athletes. It is set against the backdrop of Becketts Park and only 3 miles from the city – making it an ideal centre for students.

For horse racing fans, **the Wetherby racecourse,** opened in 1891, is the place to be. Racing began in this area with the Romans racing Arab horses. As a jump track, excitement fills the air on race days; the traditional Boxing Day event is fun for all the family.

Lots of other smaller venues can be found around Leeds, such as West Park RUFC, tennis courts at Armley and Gipton Junior football club. Wherever you are in Leeds, sport abounds.

Health-Conscious Leeds

It is little wonder that the half marathon is run so regularly: it seems Leeds folk are very health conscious. Leeds has seventeen leisure centres, fifteen swimming pools, twelve gyms and a sailing activity centre. Added to that, there are many private gyms.

In South Leeds, the John Charles South Leeds Stadium – named after the footballing legend John Charles – is a firm favourite for many. Both Charles' early years and his last years were spent at Leeds United, and in between he went on to become an international player. He was definitely an adopted 'son' of Leeds.

There are many running clubs in and around Leeds and one can always see runners both on the streets and in our country byways. The Leeds half marathon is run through the streets of Leeds. Leeds mini and junior run is free to enter. The junior is 2.5km and the mini run is 1.5km. A full marathon is run somewhere in Leeds every month.

Infamous People of Leeds

Mary Bateman – Known as the 'Yorkshire witch', she poisoned a Leeds woman in 1806. Her skeleton is still on display in the Thackray Museum today.

William Dove – Murdered his wife Harriet in 1856 by poison. The idea to murder his wife came from his dubious relationship with local 'wizard', Henry Harrison.

John Darcy – John Darcy battered William Metcalf to death in 1879. Metcalf, a retired game keeper, was eighty-five. Darcy was arrested at his lodgings in Hunslet, Leeds. His was the first execution where the press was excluded. It was dubbed a 'secret execution' by the press.

Owen Madden – Born in Leeds in 1891, he became a professional killer and an American gangster. His crime syndicate included the likes of 'Lucky' Luciano and Frank Costello. Co-founder of the famous Cotton Club in New York.

Donald Neilson – Born in Bradford, this murderer's crimes were carried out across Yorkshire, Lancashire and Shropshire. He was dubbed the 'Black Panther' by the media because he wore a black balaclava. He died in prison in 2011.

Peter Sutcliffe – 'The Yorkshire Ripper' murdered thirteen women between 1975 and 1980. Six of his victims were from Leeds, causing widespread panic among women in the area; at the time, police advised women not to walk alone at night. Sutcliffe remains in Broadmoor for the remainder of his life.

Barry Prudom – Born and brought up in Leeds, Prudom was sent to an approved school for housebreaking as a youngster. Later he enlisted as a volunteer with the Leeds-based B Squadron, 23 Air Service. Prudom's killing spree began in 1982 with the murder of a policeman near Harrogate. Three murders and two attempted murders followed. Finally, the murder of another policeman in Old Malton led to a siege of more than eleven hours, during which Prudom shot himself amid a hail of shotgun pellets from police marksmen.

Rebellious Leeds

*c.*1753 – When the first turnpikes were opened the toll payments caused such a lawless rampage that a mob demolished a gate between Leeds and Bradford. When a troop of dragoons arrived, the mob furiously attacked them, as they had the constables.

1763 – Toll bar riots caused by the expense of provisions. Such was the violence that the King's troops were called and, firing on the rioters, killed eight people, with many more injured.

1844 – A fight ensued between soldiers and the newly formed police force, after the police tried to arrest two soldiers.

1975 – During bonfire night, some 300 teenagers fought running battles with the police; two officers were critically injured after their car was stoned and crashed into a tree.

1981 – Forty-three police were injured and £2 million damage caused to shops in Chapeltown by rioting and looting youths.

1995 – Violence after police executed three warrants following a tip-off about armed robberies. Skirmishes with 100 riot police occurred when up to 150 youths set fire to cars and a pub, threw petrol bombs at police and damaged property.

How Many?

1,000

Shops in the city centre at any one time.

1,500

Wedding ceremonies take place in Leeds Town Hall per year.

8,000

People employed in the largest legal sector outside London.

8,760

The number of times each character strikes the Ivanhoe Clock, Thornton's Arcade, a year. (The clock has four figures from the novel of the same name.)

20,000

Full-time jobs in tourism per annum.

1.5 million

Overnight visitors to Leeds per year.

10 million

Day visitors to Leeds per year.

£735 million

Enters the local economy each year.

Culture Vultures

There are a plethora of theatres in Leeds:

The West Yorkshire Playhouse, which also houses the Quarry Theatre, provides theatre-goers with an alterative to the London stage for first-class entertainment. Productions so far have included *Othello*, starring Lenny Henry, and *Hamlet*, with Christopher Eccleston. *King Lear*, with Tim Pigott-Smith, was especially wonderful.

The Leeds City Varieties Music Hall, built in 1865, is a Grade II Listed building and the best surviving example of a Victorian music hall in Britain. For thirty years it was the venue for the *Good Old Days* BBC television drama, and it has seen stars like Marie Lloyd, Houdini and Charlie Chaplin. More recently, Ken Dodd opened the gala performance after an extensive refurbishment.

The Grand Theatre & Opera House was built in 1878 as a backlash to the music-hall tradition, which polite society saw as beneath them. For class-conscious Victorians there were two entrances: the front main entrance for those in the best seats and side entrances for the rest of the audience. As the home of Opera North, the Northern Ballet Theatre are frequent visitors. £31 million has been estimated for the cost of refurbishment.

The Carriageworks is a forward-thinking venue with a varied programme of theatre, with all kinds of performances to enhance and increase theatre enjoyment.

Leeds Met Gallery and Studio Theatre, part of the Faculty of Arts & Technology, shows contemporary performances.

Riley Theatre at Northern School of Contemporary Dance is a training institution offering students the opportunity to develop skills and surpass as dance artists. Various performances are produced throughout the season.

O2 Academy Leeds is a concert venue accommodating an audience of over 2,000. It has a large screen for showing national sporting events.

Odds and Ends

Roundhay Park was originally a royal hunting enclosure.

The remains of a bear pit can be seen in Cardigan Road.

A working spa bathhouse opens once a year in Gledhow Valley Woods.

Built in 1837, a seven-arch aqueduct runs for 6 miles from Eccup Reservoir, through Adel Woods and crosses Meanwood Beck.

A Moravian school at Fulneck, Pudsey, was founded in 1753 and continues today.

In 1694, Leeds was one of the first towns to have piped water.

The town's wealth was built on the woollen trade.

There are still twenty-five gas lamps in Leeds.

The Airedale terrier is the largest of all English terriers. It is named after the Aire valley, which runs from the Yorkshire Dales through Leeds and on, eventually, to the North Sea coast.

In 1916, an explosion at Barnbow Munitions factory killed thirty-five women. A memorial is to be renovated in time for the centenary.

In early 1800s when visiting England and Scotland, whilst passing through Leeds, Ralph Waldo Emerson noted:
'I observed the sheep were black and I fancied they were black sheep; no, they were begrimed with smoke.'

Quirky Buildings

Ledsham church, though about 11 miles from Leeds, is within the metropolitan borough of the City of Leeds. The name Ledsham contains elements of the original name for Loidis/Ledes. The church, dedicated to All Saints, claims to be the oldest parish church still in use. The walls of the nave and the tower base date back to the early eighth century.

There are **three towers** in Holbeck Leeds which deserve a mention if only for the sheer generosity of design by the factory owner Thomas Harding. He had the chimneys built in various styles of great Italian artists. The first tower is based on the Lamberti tower in Verona, the second is based on Giotto's marble campanile in Florence and the third is based on a Tuscan tower.

Meanwood Towers has a certain allure: it is a Victorian edifice that could not quite make up its mind what style to follow! There is a Juliet balcony, a square tower, a gabled wing and stone mullioned windows.

Mucky Leeds

In the 1890s the River Pollution Commission estimated fifty dead animals were removed from the River Aire every day.

In 1894 Alfred Orange wrote about the River Aire thus: 'The Aire is simply a huge sewer: it has the filth of Leeds in suspension'.

In 1870 there were an estimated 30,000 non-flushing privies.

A pile of human waste in Wellington Yard measured 7 metres x 2 metres and was 2 metres deep. It was reported that a local drunk had fallen in and drowned.

In 1888 a sweatshop in Leeds employed eighty men and girls; closets were the trough system and were immediately under the workshop windows.

Last but not least, The Duck and Drake situated in Kirkgate, Leeds, is known as the 'Mucky Duck'.

Great Houses of Leeds

Temple Newsam House is a Tudor-Jacobean mansion dating from the fifteenth century. It is the birthplace of Lord Darnley, ill-fated husband of Mary Queen of Scots. Temple Newsam is also famous as having the largest Knights Templar Preceptory in Yorkshire. The knights arrived in 1155.

Harewood House, Harewood village, was built between 1759 and 1771 for Edwin Lascelles. Designed by John Carr and Robert Adam, the house has gardens designed by Capability Brown and Sir Charles Barry. Much of the eighteenth-century furniture is by the famous furniture maker Thomas Chippendale. The house boasts many fine paintings.

Lotherton Hall is a beautiful Edwardian country residence and former home of the Gascoigne family, who purchased the house in 1825. There has been occupation on the site since the seventh century. The house has an extensive collection of objets d'art.

The Mansion House, Roundhay, Leeds. Situated on an elevated position and set in 700 acres in the now public Roundhay Park. Built in the classical style, of two storeys with seven bay windows and an iron portico in the centre, it is now a restaurant and café.

Two Small Houses with a Difference:
A house in Pudsey, in an area known as Buffy Lump, was called **Castle House**; it stood on an old packhorse route. It had a 'kissing stone' near the front door. According to local folklore, if you kissed the kissing stone and made a wish, your true love would be made known.

There is a little house in Aberford known as **Demi Luce** (the Luce is taken from the half pike on the Gascoigne heraldry). There are only four rooms, and the two attic rooms had bells. It is possible that the house was originally a gatehouse. Lilliput Lane Cottages have made a miniature of it.

Mysteries

The Crown & Fleece closed in the 1930s but two carved skulls remained on the outside wall until 1974. Then they vanished. Then they reappeared! The skulls first appeared in the eighteenth century, and supposedly belong to two men who hid in the pub's stables to avoid being called up into the army. While hiding, they suffocated in the hayloft.

Sometimes, the Town Hall clock strikes thirteen. It doesn't happen often, and it's usually at night, but not always. No one knows when or why, only that it does.

According to legend, four lions at the entrance to the Town Hall occasionally get up and move; the only proof that this happens is that the lions never return to their original stance. There are always slight variations in their expressions and position.

Situated in an isolated area between the River Aire and the Leeds-Liverpool Canal, local legend states the Abbey Inn, Newlay Lane, has a tunnel running between it and Kirkstall Abbey. As an inn, its history can only be traced back to 1826; prior to that records show it as a farmhouse. The mind races to think why there had to be a tunnel to the monks...

Fancy That!

Architect Benjamin Latrobe, born at Fulneck, Leeds, remodeled the iconic White House and the Library of Congress in Washington D.C.

In 1807, Mrs Siddons of the York Theatre Company came to Leeds to play Lady Macbeth. When, as Lady Macbeth, she was playing the sleep-walking scene, a boy from the company marched on to the stage with a jug of 'porter', despite many attempts to stop him, to the huge annoyance of the great actress and to the amusement of the audience. Mrs Siddons' annoyance was further increased when, as she was taking the poison during that key scene, a lout in the gods bawled, 'Sup it up, lass'. These unpleasant occurrences the tragedy queen could not forgive and, as the curtain came down, she was heard to exclaim 'Farewell, ye brutes'!

In 1795, Dr John Aiken – better known as a man of letters than a physician – noted that: 'The markets of Leeds are supplied with all kinds of provisions. The price of best beef is 5d to 6d per pound, mutton and veal 4.5d per pound – about half a penny cheaper than York.'

This and That

The original Leeds Infirmary was built by subscription in 1768, together with a workhouse, almshouses and a charity school.

Luddism spread to Leeds in 1812 when numerous factories were attacked.

In March 1941, Leeds suffered its heaviest bombing raid.

Waddingtons, the famous board-game manufacturers, supplied boards to service personnel held in German prisoner-of-war camps. They inserted a map of Europe printed on silk to help escapees.

Arriving at Leeds Museum in 1824, the Egyptian mummy Natsef-Amun was the only Egyptian mummy to survive a German air attack during the Second World War.

In February 1947, 1,450 men, equipped with 174 snow-shifting vehicles and shovels and forty snow ploughs, worked to clear the streets of Leeds.

A minister once walked 20 miles in the snow to take a divine service in Leeds.

In February 1962, Leeds City Station was closed because of the danger of falling glass due to a hurricane.

In 1962, whilst the hurricane winds were in full force, Otley Market closed for the first time in thirty years. One brave soul set out his wares in the shelter of the Buttercross; he lost hundreds of eggs!

Lasting Impressions

In Leeds parish church there is an effigy of a knight in chain-mail armour, with plate knee caps, sword and shield. It is preserved in stunningly carved limestone. The coat of arms on the shield show him to be of the Steyton (Stainton) family. The effigy is dated not later than Edwards II's time, or about 1320. In the reign of Edward III, the knight's kinswoman, Elizabeth Stainton, was Prioress of Kirklees Priory.

Dating from around 1800, 'The Wensleydale Lad' was a popular song in Leeds. It described the experiences of a naïve young dalesman who had come to Leeds to enjoy the excitement of one of the town's great fairs, possibly that of the 8-9 November, when people stood around Briggate to get themselves hired as servants for the coming year.

The Knights Templar held many assets in Leeds. Properties in Briggate comprised of inns, tenant cottages and land-strips, tenant farms and crofts further afield; they also included the village of Colton, Whitkirk church and land at Skelton and Halton. Their preceptory at Temple Newsam was one of the largest in Yorkshire.

Bits and Pieces

Parlington Triumphal Arch, Aberford, which originally led to Parlington Hall, is thought to be a copy of an arch to Titus or Constantine in Rome. The inscription on the Arch reads 'Liberty in N. America'.

A document attributed to Sir Thomas Gascoigne regarding the arch states:

'To that virtue which for a series of years resisted oppression and by a glorious race rescued its country and millions from slavery.' (Abbreviated)

Aberford is a midway point between London and Edinburgh, being 200 miles in either direction when the Great North Road was the main throughfare.

The Swan Hotel at Aberford was a staging post for travellers.

After the Battle of Towton, Aberford, remnants of the Lancastrian army are said to have crossed the River Cock on the bodies of fallen comrades. Cock Beck/river bisects Aberford.

The Arabian Horse in Aberford is thought to be the only pub with this name; it derives from the arrival in Leeds of Arabian horsestock for the racehorse bloodline. The Arabs who delivered the horses were stranded in Aberford by bad weather and were the focus of attention for miles around.

Must be the Air!

Instances of great longevity in Leeds:

	Age	Year Died
Juno Kitchingman Esq	115	1510
Thomas Barnard	103	1698
A 'poor woman'	102	1699
Robert Oglesby	114	1768
Grace Barnard	101	1804
Eva Randall	100	1830

Ancient Monuments and Buildings

Leeds has 2,330 listed buildings and monuments; here are a handful of them:

Adel Church of St John the Baptist, 1150–1170 (Grade I Listed)

Lambert's Arcade, sixteenth-century timber-framed house and workshop (Grade II Listed)

Sagar Place, Headingley, early nineteenth-century coursed squared grit-stone cottage (Grade II Listed)

Cottages, Headingley, *c.* 1860, in Gothic revival style (Grade II Listed)

Cookridge, sixteenth-century aisled barn (Grade II Listed)

Armley Park, two Victorian ornamental plaques (Grade II Listed)

Bramley, *c.*1500, timber-framed aisled hall, later encased in stone (Grade II Listed)

Aberford, 1844, former Gascoigne Almshouses (Grade II Listed)

Armley Jail, 1847, outwardly designed like a castle (Grade II Listed). It was for many years notorious as a 'hanging jail': around ninety-three prisoners were executed, some, in the early years, publically. The infamous burglar, escape artist and murderer Charles 'Charlie' Peace was probably the most notorious prisoner to lose his life at Leeds, in February 1879

And not so ancient!
A telephone kiosk, 1935, Oxford Place, Leeds (Grade II Listed)

A post box, 1936, bearing ER VIII, Cookridge Lane, Leeds (Grade II Listed)

Ghosts

City Varieties Theatre has two ghosts who call this home: one plays piano late at night, the other is a lady who moves around in a zone of cold air.

At the **Cardigan Arms** pub, ladies beware: an elderly lady with straight grey hair has been glimpsed in a mirror or otherwise seen in the toilets!

At a **Conservative Club** an apparition materialised by the doorway. It could be clearly seen on the CCTV network. It vanished after a few minutes, but has since reappeared.

Temple Newsam House has a number of ghostly apparitions, which include a monk in brown robes, a Knight Templar, a small boy and a lady in blue. Screams have been heard in the south wing and the sounds of something – or someone – being dragged across the floor.

Beneath the steps of **Leeds Town Hall** is the old prison; the murderer Charlie Peace (pictured opposite) is said to haunt the cells.

At the **Abbey Inn**, Newlay, three ghosts may be found: a lady in grey, an enigmatic gentleman in a cloak and a man in a Guy Fawkes' type hat. From the cellar comes the sound of a gaggle of girls giggling.

Bodysnatchers

The Rose and Crown Yard stood on the site of the present Queens Arcade in Briggate. The yard was occupied by Morley Temperance Hotel on the left and the Rose and Crown Hotel on the right. Beyond lay a range of shops: joiners; cabinetmakers; a coffee roaster; fishmongers; tobacconists; and plumbers. It was here in 1831 that James Norton was arrested when trying to place a box containing the body of Robert Hudson, recently removed from East Ardsley churchyard by body-snatchers, on to the Edinburgh coach.

On 11 November 1831 a box arrived at the Bull and Mouth Hotel, Leeds, on the coach of the Duke of Leeds' company from Manchester. Addressed to 'The Rev. Geneste, Hull, per Selby. To be left until called for. Glass, keep this side up.' A nosey servant opened the box (possibly due to the unsavory aroma) and discovered the bodies of a woman and a child inside. Several people stood trial at York for the crime.

I wonder if the celebrated Dr Robert Knox (Edinburgh) still accepted bodies of unknown providence after the Burke and Hare trial of 1828?

Museums, Galleries and Attractions

Leeds City Art Gallery, The Headrow. Free admission
This art gallery has an impressive collection including historic paintings by Elizabeth Butler and the atmospheric Atkinson Grimshaw, and sculptures by Barbara Hepworth and Antony Gormley.

The Royal Armouries Museum, Crown Point. Free admission
The home of the National Museum of Arms and Armour has six main galleries housing 5,000 objects ranged over two floors, though there are five floors in total. The museum has a Hall of Steel with a display of 2,500 objects, conservation workshops, libraries and conference facilities, shop and café.

Leeds City Museum, Millennium Square. Free admission
The City Museum has four floors of exciting galleries. Discover the ancient world of Egypt and the 3,000-year-old mummy. Explore the story of how Leeds has been shaped over thousands of years. Changing gallery exhibitions make this a worthwhile visit many times over.

Armley Mills Industrial Museum, Canal Road, Armley
One of the largest textile museums in the world, it tells the story of manufacturing in Leeds from the eighteenth century. The history of the site goes back to 1707 when it was a fulling mill. Fulling is the beating of cloth in order to 'felt' it. The mill was sold twice before Benjamin Gott bought it in 1804, rebuilding it in fireproof materials. It is Gott's mill that we see today.

Abbey House Museum, Kirkstall

Situated just outside the city centre, away from the busy city, this offers a riverside setting for picnic and walks. The museum captures life in the twelfth century for the monks of Kirkstall Abbey. You can learn when they prayed, cooked and slept and even see a reconstruction of the laybrother's toilet! The abbey grounds provide the setting for plays in the summer.

Lotherton Hall, Aberford

The Edwardian house and estate provides a glimpse into the luxury lifestyle of the Gascoigne family, the previous owners of the house. The house is filled with stunning objets d' art, paintings and china. Within the extensive grounds is a bird garden, formal gardens and woodland walks.

Temple Newsam, off Selby Road, Leeds

Temple Newsom has something for everyone; an impressive house which was, for 300 years, the home of the Ingram family. Thirty rooms offer the visitor a peek into the life of top drawer English society. With furniture by Thomas Chippendale, lavish textiles, silver and delicate pottery, the visitor can easily be overwhelmed with the opulence. Added to that there is a rare-breed farm and miles of walks.

Thwaite Mills, Stourton, Leeds

This restored working water mill, rebuilt between 1823 and 1825, is situated between the River Aire and the Aire & Calder Navigation. The site contains a two-storey building for the mill with an attic, an engineers' workshop, a row of cottages for the workers, a warehouse and stables. The mill manager had a large house, known as Thwaite House: it now houses exhibitions relating to the mill.

Thomas Chippendale House, Otley

The Chippendale Society was founded in 1965 to mark the impact Thomas Chippendale had on furniture design. The society organise events, lectures, study days and visits to places connected to Chippendale. An annual dinner is held to commemorate the baptism of Otley's most famous son. Chippendale House is not a registered museum.

Night Vision

1192 – Late one cold January afternoon, a Belgian monk reported seeing, '... a kind of terrible fire that filled the entire Northern part of the sky'.

1197 – Similar sights were reported in the North of England and would certainly have been seen in the area of Leeds. It was an *aurora borealis* and was blamed for the terrible famine of 1197.

1938 – Another *aurora borealis* was visible throughout the county on 25 and 26 January.

1949 – ... And yet another, oddly enough also on 25 and 26 January.

2008 – July brought several reports of strange red and/or white lights moving slowly over Leeds. There was also a report of a 'witch' terrifying a woman.

Leeds/Yorkshire Sayings

To addle – to work or earn.

Hoddit – to hold.

Mistal – cow byre or cowshed.

Ah can't thoil it – not worth spending money on an item.

It's nut jannock – just a small amount.

Nah, ah didna own you – not recognized.

Ahim starved to death – to be very cold. From the Anglo-Saxon verb *stearfan*, 'to die', still used in German as *sterben*.

To sam – to gather or pick, from the Anglo-Saxon *samnian*, similar to German *sammeln*.

Nobbut – 'nought/nothing but', derived from the Anglo-Saxon *nan-beatan*. Nobbut was recently popularized by Matt Lucas in the television series *Little Britain*.

Go laiking – to go out to play.

Yolk – corruption of *mjolk* meaning 'milk'. In Leeds, as late as the 1940s, milkmen delivering milk by pony and trap would shout 'yoooolk'. Both words come from old Scandinavian – a leftover from the Viking invasions, perhaps?

Arran – spider.

Fent – remnant of cloth, derived from fender, to split.

Buffet – stool.

Fumery – a dish made from wheat, from 'froment', meaning 'wheat'. All words from Norman French, probably dating from the Norman invasion of 1066.

Parks

Leeds is rich in green areas and parks – Leeds City Council manages about 4,000 hectares of parks and open spaces. There are eight major parks in Leeds and many community parks and playgrounds. Leeds has a team of motorcycle rangers patrolling the open areas. The main parks are:

Golden Acre Park

Gotts/Armley Park

Otley Chevin

Middleton Park

Roundhay Park

Temple Newsam Estate

Lotherton Hall Estate

Kirkstall Abbey Estate

Leeds in Days Gone By

Kirkstall in Days Gone By

Flora and Fauna

There are over 1,000 tree preservation orders in Leeds. Areas of special interest include:

Fairburn Ings is an extensive area of marsh and open water. It is of national importance for wild waterfowl. During the winter months it is home to shoveler ducks, whooper swans and the pochard – to name but a few. There are five bird hides – a must for bird-watching enthusiasts.

Townclose Nature Reserve boasts a mixture of habitats supporting a diverse range of plant and animal life, including bee orchids, six-spot burnet moths and a variety of grasses.

Rodley Nature Reserve is in the heart of Leeds and was created on a floodplain. It is designed to bring wetland wildlife into the area. On the lagoon, both little grebe and tufted duck can be seen, while the reedbeds encourage the reed warblers, water rails and kingfishers. Many different kinds of dragonfly can be seen in the warm summer months. The seed fields bring in linnets and red bunting.

Kirkstall Valley Nature Reserve takes in Bramley Fall, Hawksworth Woods and Burley Mills, among other areas along the valley. Here fox cubs roam, and the rabbits run: all kinds of wildlife can be seen for those of a patient nature. Birds abound, and the sharp-eyed may spot a warbler or the shy thrush. There are also a myriad of butterflies and moths to be found here.

Bat box and badger monitoring is carried out in a number of locations. Three species of bats are found in Leeds: common pipistrelle, Daubenton's and brown long-eared.

Artistic Connections

The celebrated artist **J.M.W. Turner** visited Harewood House as a young man of twenty-two. He painted magnificent paintings whilst there, many of which remain in the collection of Harewood House today.

Thomas Girtin, a watercolour artist who died tragically young, was a visitor to Harewood House and stayed near Leeds on occasions.

The photographer **Roger Fenton** also spent time at Harewood village, taking some memorable photographs.

John Atkinson Grimshaw, a true Leeds artist, was famous for his atmospheric paintings.

Damian Hirst attended Leeds College of Art and is best remembered for his dead animals preserved in formaldehyde. In 2008 he sold a complete show for a staggering £111 million.

Businesses in Leeds

Leeds is one of the top twenty-five cities for business, and is one of the largest business and financial centres outside London. It is home to a rich diversity of businesses with particular strengths in the legal sector, which is the largest outside of London.

Leeds covers a wide variety of activities in manufacturing, with some 1,800 companies. These include specialized engineering, food, drinks, chemicals, medical technology with DePuy International/medical apparatus and sweeties. Lever Faberge provides the beauty products to keep the population looking lovely, while Agfa are at the leading edge of world print and graphics.

Overall, 36,000 people are employed, generating over £15 billion per annum.

And then there are the creative industries, which include: publishing, television, architecture and the Performing Arts.

Biotech manufacturing includes household names such as Samsung; the University of Leeds has founded three biotechnology companies.

Some of the biggest high street names have based their headquarters here in Leeds; among them are First Direct Line, Halifax Direct and ASDA, which, as part of the giant retailer Walmart, has a head office in Leeds.

University of Leeds Hon. Degrees

The Leeds honorary degree system can be traced back to 1904; during that year Sir Edward Elgar, composer, and Tempest Anderson, an ophthalmic surgeon, were among the recipients.

Other notables, among hundreds, are:
Herbert Henry Asquith (LLD)

Sir Almroth Edward Wright (Dsc)

David Lloyd George (LLD)

Dame Ellen Musson (LLD)

Henry Moore (DLitt)

Barbara Hepworth (DLitt)

Dame Fanny Waterman (MA)

Nikolaus Pevsner (DLitt)

Jeremy Paxman (LLD)

Leeds Metropolitan University

Leeds Met, as it is commonly called, gained university status in 1992, but can trace its roots back to 1824. The university has three main campus sites, two in Leeds and one in Bhopal, India.

Notable recent awards of honorary degrees wen to:

Geoffrey Boycott OBE, cricketer

Sir George Martin CBE , composer and record producer

James Caan, entrepreneur

'Sprouting' Leeds: The Coronation of King George VI

1936 saw the abdication of one king and the ascendance of another – King George VI. With this momentous event came a huge planting of trees. Many were planted in the Leeds area; perhaps the most important was by HRH the Princess Royal. The planting ceremony took place in Crabtree Lane, East Keswick. She planted a red twigged lime. Twelve other trees were planted at the same time.

Other places where tree planting took place included Park Lane Estate, Guisley; Hall Park, Horsforth; the public pleasure grounds, Ilkley; St Peter's churchyard; and in the vicarage garden, Morley; and at Scaur Bank, Wetherby.

Beech trees, both red and green, oaks, limes and red and white horse-chestnut trees were among the favourite choices, but only one lovely double lilac tree was planted, at St Peter's churchyard.

Overall, hundreds of trees were planted for this coronation. Over the years, Leeds has remained very green, with masses of trees being planted for various occasions.

Festivals and Events

The Leeds Music Festival – The first festival was held at Temple Newsam in 1999 with the Red Hot Chilli Peppers; in 2003 the festival moved to its current home at Bramham Park. Past highlights have included the Kaiser Chiefs in 2006 and Guns 'n Roses in 2010. The festival is a forum for raw and unsigned talented bands.

Opera in the Park – As the name implies, this is an evening of classical music. Held at Temple Newsam House, a glorious outdoor venue, picnics and stars from the world of opera, as well as a marvellous firework finale, all combine to produce an evening to remember.

Party in the Park – Also held at Temple Newsam House, after the opera on Saurday evening, the Sunday is for partying with a line-up of British pop stars. With an offer of free tickets, you have to be quick off the mark. However, if you miss out on free tickets you can listen to a live broadcast of the event on Radio Aire.

Leeds International Pianoforte Competition – This was founded in 1961 by Dame Fanny Waterman DBE DMus FRCM. The competition is held every three years and offers young talented pianists a chance to advance their careers. The initial stages are held at the Great Hall, and those who reach the finals have the opportunity to play a concerto with an orchestra in Leeds Town Hall.

The Leeds West Indian Carnival – Held in and around Chapeltown, this is the longest-running West Indian Carnival in Europe: it began in 1967. It is a three-day event, which starts and ends in Potternewton Park. From 2008, both a carnival king and queen have been chosen.

The Leeds International Film Festival – This is the largest British film festival held outside of London. It is held in November at various venues throughout Leeds and shows over 200 films from around the world.

Leeds Mela/Bollywood in the Park – Roundhay Park is a showcase for Asian culture. It features a wide array of stalls, food and entertainment.

Leeds Food and Drink Festival – Over three days, this event is held across Leeds City Centre, at sites including Millennium Square (which hosts over 100 stalls), Briggate and The Victoria Quarter. A variety of chefs showcase their work in the Theatre Kitchen and other restaurants across the city.

Leeds Shakespeare Festival – Held at Kirkstall Abbey, this is a summer must! Two plays are performed, one tragedy and one comedy. A household name is always enticed to perform with the regular company; in the past notables have included Wayne Sleep, Norman Pace and Sean Brosnan.

The German Market – Millennium Square, Leeds, is one of the most established German markets in the UK. The market has over forty authentic German traders in wooden chalet-type stalls, all dressed up for Christmas – a delight to see.

Musicians

Leeds bands include:

A Day For Heroes	Punk/metal band
A-GP-2C	Indie rock covers band
The Alaskans	Rock'n'Roll
Anarcadia	Progressive thrash band
Arizona Bay	Grunge revivalists
The Wolves	R&B/Funk

And singers:

Phoebe Katis	Folk/Pop/Jazz
Harry Callahan	Hardcore band

Filmed in Leeds

Leeds has been a prime location for film and television producers. The television detective series *A Touch of Frost* starring David Jason, a long-running series, was shot at various locations across Leeds.

For football fanatics, ***The Damned United***, starring Michael Sheen and loosely based on the football manager Brian Clough during his tenure at Leeds United, sometimes shows Leeds in a poor light.

In an altogether different mood, ***A Passionate Woman***, starring Billie Piper, was based on a true story of a 1950s housewife who fell in love with her neighbour. Leeds has been used as a location for numerous films over the years, and the people of the city have made both cast and crew most welcome – long may it last!

Heroes of Leeds

Queen Victoria established the Victoria Cross in 1854. There is a memorial in Leeds at the junction of the Headrow and Park Square to Victoria Cross holders who were either born or died in Leeds. The metal for the medals comes from Russian guns captured in the Crimean War. There are seventeen recipients of the Victoria Cross from Leeds. Of the many, I have chosen one example from each conflict or place.

The First World War

Harry M. Daniels, Company Sergeant Major, 2nd Battalion Rifle Brigade (Prince Consort's Own), died in France, March 1915. When his unit was ordered to advance to the German trenches across No-Man's-Land, he rushed out first to cut through the barbed wire for his comrades. He later died from his wounds, having been shot almost immediately.

Charles Hull, Private, 21st Lancers (Empress of India's), died in India in September 1915. He received the Victoria Cross after rescuing an officer from certain death at the hands of tribesmen: taking the officer up behind him on his own horse, he galloped to safety.

The Second World War

Arthur Louis Aaron, Flight Sergeant, Volunteer Reserve, RAF 218 squadron, died in Italy in August 1943. He sustained horrific injuries during a flight but, despite terrible pain, he helped to bring his plane down in a belly-landing in darkness by writing directions and instructions to his bomb aimer.

The Boer War

Alfred Atkinson, Sergeant 1st Battalion, The Yorkshire Regiment (Alexander, Princess of Wales' Own), died in South Africa in February 1900. During the battle of Paardeberg, he went out seven times to obtain water for the wounded.

Waikato-Hauhau, Maori War, New Zealand

John Pearson, Private, 8th Hussars (The King's Royal Irish), died in New Zealand in September 1863. Charging, under converging fire, into an enemy camp of two batteries, Private Pearson's squadron captured two enemy guns.

TO THE MEMORY OF ALL THOSE
CITIZENS OF LEEDS WHO SERVED IN
THE GREAT WAR 1914 - 1918

IN PARTICULAR WE REMEMBER
WITH PRIDE THE SOLDIERS OF
THE LEEDS RIFLES AND THE LEEDS PALS

"I prayed to God to help me, and he has answered my prayer"
15/456 Lance Corporal Sydney Hicks
A Company, the Leeds Pals

Things to do in Leeds

Visit the Victorian Quarter, Lands Lane or Briggate to do some shopping, or, to look for something really different, try the Corn Exchange.

Don't miss the craft centre below the steps at Leeds Library (the library is also worth a look just for the tiled hall alone).

Take a train to Ilkley and have a splash in the Ilkley Lido, followed up with a walk by the River Wharfe.

Visit Goodalls ice-cream parlour at Tong village.

Kirkstall Abbey, once home to Cistercian monks, is a must when visiting Leeds.

For a really good coffee and snack, go to Millennium Square, the location of several popular cafés, and a great place in winter to watch the ice-skaters fly by.

Watch a Turneresque sunset on Otley Chevin.

Pop into The Loch Fyne restaurant in the Old Post Office on City Square if you prefer fish to meat. Or, for a good Thai meal, try the Thai Edge restaurant, Calverly Street, just below the Leeds LGI.

Take a walk along the canal ending with a pint at the old-fashioned, real-ale pub the Abbey Inn, Pollard Lane, Newlay.

Visit The Oceana, Leeds' largest nightclub, which has seven separate themed rooms.

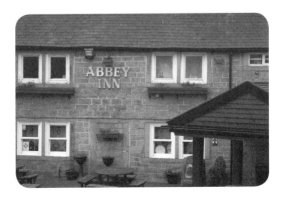

Hotels

There are at least seventy-five hotels in Leeds plus many more located on the outlying districts of the metropolis that is Leeds. The Queens Hotel, adjacent to the railway station, is a famous landmark in Leeds. It is a favourite for 'launches' of every kind. It has an old-fashioned glamour and hidden secrets beneath its grand Portland stone exterior. A hidden world of tunnels and vaulted cavernous rooms lie beneath the stately rooms. Stalactites hang glistening on the walls and a door opens directly to the River Aire. This part of the hotel is a far cry from the genteel rooms above.

De Vere Oulton Hall Hotel has one of the grandest entrances of the Leeds hotels. A Grade II Listed building, it oozes grace and charm and is just the place to go for a special afternoon tea or a splash of champagne on the terrace. Don't be fooled into thinking everything is old-fashioned: it houses a spa and fitness suite and boasts a golf course and practice range.

The Hilton Leeds has seen its fair share of newspaper headlines. Once the favourite hotel for stars performing at the Leeds theatres, it has seen hordes of screaming fans flood its entrance.

Otley Chevin Hotel and Spa is set in the rolling countryside between Leeds and Otley. Walk in the secluded grounds and unspoilt woodlands. The lakeside restaurant and Sonas Spa helps you to relax and be pampered, far from the cares of the world. There are also many budget hotels in and around Leeds city centre.

Ditties of Leeds

Come listen to my tragedy, good people young & old,
It's of a dreadful story, to you I will unfold,
Concerning a young gentleman, William was his name,
Killed by his deceitful girl, whose lover did take the
blame.

The Judge began his verdict, saying ,'I believe what I am
told.
'Your confession means you'll meet your end. May God
take pity on your soul.
'At Armley Jail tonight you'll hang, upon the gallows high,
'For the killing of young William, on the stroke of twelve
you'll die.'

So to the cells this man was led, his punishment to await,
And there he sat, with head held high, preparing for his fate.
'At Armley Jail tonight I'll hang, upon the gallows high
'That she may live, my love so fair, on the stroke of
twelve I'll die.'

In her grief the doleful girl did climb the clocktower tall,
And looked about until upon the jail her eyes did fall.
'And now the chimes they do strike twelve, so quick I'll
end my life,
'For I no longer wish to live, less he be by my side.'

The Judge still sits in Leeds Town Hall, & God He sits on
high.The poor girl's broken bones, under cold crossed-
roads they lie.
And if the chimes again strike twelve, 'tis said her bones
will rise,
And walk the steps of Leeds Town Hall, again until sunrise.

The Ballad of Leeds Town Hall, Attributed to a Leeds wife

The Tune is 'the Bleeding Heart', & c.

ALAS! what times here be
For men to live so sinfully; Nothing but wickedness doth reign
In people's hearts, we find it plain;

The Devil prompts men unto sin, And to amend they'll not begin, Till Justice overtakes them straight; Then they repent when 'tis too late; God grant us Grace, and keep us free From Murther and Adultery!

But now my subject to incite, It doth my muses sore affright; And forceth me to shed a tear, For me to write what you shall hear. 'Tis of a young man, I may say, Which did his parents not obey; But like a crafty cunning elf, Despis'd his friends, ruin'd himself; God grant us Grace, &c.

This man to lust was so inclin'd, And for to satisfie his mind, Did covit straight another's wife, For which no doubt he'll lose his life; Her husband being gone to sea, He often kept her company, And night and day was at her still, His wicked mind for to fullfill: God grant us Grace, &c.

Alas! quoth she, this must not be, My husband being now at sea, And I but lately married am, Pray don't a weak woman trapan: Oh, my dear, there's none shall know, My tender love, which I will show; If thou lov'st me, as I do thee, Thou ever shall live happily; God grant us Grace, and keep us free.

From *Murther and Adultery*

Picture Credits

Photographs are by the author unless otherwise stated. I thank all those who have assisted with photographs – and special thanks to Barrie Colton for making good my own photographs!

Page:

2. Leeds looking westwards, towards the city

3. Coat of arms

7. Rear of Leeds Civic Hall, Portland Gate; Harvey Nicholls luxury department store

9. Leeds map of 1725; Leeds map of 1866

11. Briggate, 'road to the bridge', in 1900

13. St John the Baptist church, Adel. Built in 1150, it lies near an ancient road from Ilkley to Tadcaster; Wetherby Bridge (David Pickersgill)

15. Cristo de la Concordia, the largest statue of Jesus Christ in the world (Jimmy Gile); Caerphilly Castle. Building began in 1268. It is the second largest castle in Europe (Tony Hisgett)

17. Hicks Mill, seen in a rural setting amid farm buildings; Sugarwell Mill (left) and Kippax Mill (right); a tower-type mill, now part of a Leeds hotel

19. Henry Moore's renowned 'Reclining Woman' residing outside the City Art Gallery; a Victorian figure overlooking Leeds city centre

21. From her high vantage point, the imposing statue of Queen Victoria gazes across Hyde Park Moor; the metal sculpture of a dragonfly on Leeds waterfront

23. North Beach, Durban, South Africa (Lesli Lundgren)

25. The Town Hall, Utah (Utah History Society)

26. Statue of the Black Prince sited approximately where de Lacy Castle stood. The old main post office can be seen in the background

27. The Leeds-Liverpool Canal, still an important waterway for the city

29. The River Aire. Warehouses have become high-rise, up-market dwellings, well away from the floods; Bramley Fall lock on the Leeds-Liverpool Canal, scene of devastation during gale-force winds

31. Leeds Mosque, one of several to grace the city; a Puritan chapel at Bramhope. Built in 1649, although now redundant, it was well used but thought never to have been consecrated

33. Charlotte Bronte, one of the famous Bronte sisters from Haworth (The University of Texas Libraries)

35. Prizes (SXC)

37. Bust of Prince Edward, Prince of Wales, in Leeds Town Hall; statue of Queen Victoria situated in Leeds Town Hall; Leeds Civic Hall, built in 1931 with money raised from a government fund to employ the jobless.

39. Benjamin Gott's home, now used as a clubhouse for the golf course; Joseph Priestley (left) and John Harrison (right), two of the 'Men of City Square' installed to celebrate the elevation of Leeds to City status

41. Leeds General Infirmary, working towards the health of the city; statue of Titus Salt in Roberts Park (Jungpioneer, http://creativecommons.org/licenses/by-sa/3.0/deed.en)

43. Robert Blackburn's Monoplane – certainly a magnificent man with his flying machine (By kind permission of the B.A.E. Systems Heritage Centre)

45. Writers of Leeds (SXC)

47. Leeds City Varieties. Music hall is still strong in Leeds, with the ghosts of a bygone age watching the stage (Leeds Theatres & Opera House Ltd)

49. Leeds produces many sporting stars (Body Cuts 5, SXC)

51. Headingley Stadium looking rather like a lopsided wedding cake!; Kirkstall Leisure Centre, one of many throughout the city

53. South Leeds Stadium, renamed the John Charles Centre after the great sportsman who made Leeds his home

55. Mary Bateman skeleton: a gruesome end, but lasting notoriety (thanks to the Thackray Museum for allowing access to Mary Bateman's skeleton)

57. Leeds Police, keeping us safe from rebellion

59. The wonderful building of Leeds Town Hall, dating from 1853/8 and designed by Cuthbert Brodrick; the spectacular chiming clock in Thornton's Arcade

61. The Grand Theatre, which certainly lives up to its name, being grand in every way (Leeds Theatres & Opera House Ltd)

63. The Old Bear Pit, a grisly reminder of what passed as 'sport' for our forebears; one of the twenty-five gas lamps in Leeds

65. Two of the Italianate chimneys at Holbeck; beautiful designs for a dirty job

67. The famous Duck & Drake pub stands on an old thoroughfare of Leeds

69. Lotherton Hall – former home to the Gascoigne family; the Mansion House, now available for public enjoyment; the State Bedroom, Harewood House. The wall was moved to accommodate the bed

71. One of the two lions guarding Leeds Town Hall

73. Rolling Easter eggs on the White House Lawn, 1914 (Library of Congress, LC-DIG-hec-03961)

75. An Egyptian Mummy in all its glory with exquisite workmanship to be seen on the coffin (Lypsippos)

77. Leeds parish church became a Minster with a service of dedication on 2 September 2012 in recognition of its civic role, in the year of the Queen's Diamond Jubilee

79. Parlington Triumphal Arch (Brian Hull); the old Coaching Inn, Aberford

81. A Leeds resident celebrates ninety well-spent years (2005)

83. Listed cottages in Headingley; Gascoigne Almshouses (Brian Hull); a Victorian plaque, Gotts Park. A full-time job keeping the ivy away!

85. Leeds Town Hall. The steps hide the prison beneath; Charles Peace

87. The execution of Burke

91. The *aurora borealis*, or Northern Lights, above Bear Lake, Alaska (Senior Airman Joshua Strang)

93. Folk keep alive the old sayings (sketch by Brian Goodall)

95. Golden Acre Park; Roundhay Park; Gotts Park

96. GPO building; New Briggate in 1900

97. Boar Lane; Bond Street

99. Kirkstall (courtesy of the Library of Congress, LC-DIG-ppmsc-09037)

101. Snowdrops herald the coming of spring and countryside walks on the Meanwood trail

103. An intricate mosaic sign for the Leeds Collage of Art; South Front at Harewood House where many notable artists have been inspired

105. Business is the beating heart of Leeds city centre (SXC)

107. Tempest Anderson, a leading exponent in the field of eye surgery (© Tempest Anderson Yorkshire Philosophical Society)

109. His Royal Highness King George VI: a gentle manner belied his strengths; an explosion of tree planting in 1936/7 occured throughout Leeds

111. Leeds Festival (Ian Wilson)

113. Kirkstall Abbey, an atmospheric setting for Shakespeare's plays; Millennium Square Gardens has a cosmopolitan feel with cafés and restaurants. The upper square is a focal point for festivals, ice-skating with a large screen for national events.

115. Music (SXC)

117. *King Ralph,* starring Peter O'Toole, John Goodman and Richard Griffiths (among others), was filmed on the South Terrace at Harewood House

119. Homage to those we can never repay for their service

121. Looking towards the Corn Exchange from Duncan Street; Leeds City Museum, formally The Leeds Institute; a leisurely canal walk to the Abbey Inn for a well-earned drink

123. The Queens Hotel, an elegant Leeds hotel built in Portland stone, adjacent to the busy railway station